# BULLYPROOF

## How to Stop Bullying and Gain Black Belt Confidence

### JAMES KERR

### Karate Master and Dad

ISBN:1469951223
ISBN-13: 978-1469951225

# DEDICATION

This book is for my son Phillipe...and all young kids like him. He's 11 years old, cute, and happy-go-lucky. He's also a bit clumsy and little nerdy. He sometimes trips on his own feet and tumbles to the ground like a sack of potatoes.

I hope he blossoms into a fine young athlete someday. But if he never does, that's OK, too.

In the meantime, I want to do what I can to help him grow and be strong. I want him to feel good about himself and to walk with confidence. I don't want him to be bullied. I don't want him to feel inferior.

This book is designed to give him and other children the skills and the energy to be safe. I know I can't guarantee him a blissful life. But I can make sure he's equipped as best as possible for the challenges he will face as a youngster.

For him and other children like him, I have a simple message: There's is a tiger inside you. I call it Black Belt Confidence. This book will show you how to wake up that tiger and make the world yours. I will show you that you've had it all along. You just need to get it back.

# ACKNOWLEDGMENT

Thank you to my students at Smart Karate who inspire me every day by growing stronger and more confident.

# CONTENTS

*CONTACT US AT:*

*www.facebook.com/bullyproofkids*

# YOU CAN

There's nothing tricky about the things I'm going to teach you. Anyone can do it. I once worked with a child who was paralyzed at birth and over time learned how to do forward rolls like a champion. And I have seen students with Down syndrome smash through wooden boards and earn their black belts.

If you're reading this book, then you already have what it takes. And if you don't believe me, then just promise me one thing: You will try. If you just try as best you can, I will take care of the rest.

# WEAR A SMILE

Before we go any further, do me a favor. Smile. Even if it's just the tiny corners of your mouth, smile. Fake it if you have to. Do what it takes, but give me a nice smile. Turn that frown around!

If you want to have some fun, try smiling at yourself in the mirror. Don't think about how you look, just give yourself a nice, big toothy smile. Like I said, fake it if you have to. You will quickly discover how quickly you can 'fake' something (That's a black belt skill!) and how good it feels inside to smile at yourself.

Here's a good exercise: Find a parent or a friend and have a laughing session. First you laugh, then the other person laughs, and so on. It's OK if the laugh is forced. Just fake it. In fact, the less sincere the laugh, the funnier it is for both of you. Three people taking turns laughing obnoxiously works well, too.

7

Why smile? Well, for starters it will make you feel better. It's true. Second, you will look friendlier. Mean looking people always get picked on. Genuinely happy looking people are less likely to be bothered.

## STAND TALL

If you appear weak, you will get picked on. The bad guys always look for the easy target. You never see lions hunting the strongest-looking zebra. They always go for the one with three legs. This is true at school and it's true on the street. If you look like an easy target, then you ARE a target.

Fortunately, with some training, you can appear bigger and stronger than you are.

Here's how: Stand in front of a full-length mirror and notice your posture. Are you bent? Hunched? Chest caved in? Then you look like an easy target.

I see many introverted children, living their days looking at the ground, drawn within themselves. It's so sad.

Here's an instant fix: Stand tall as if someone is measuring your height. Really stand as tall as possible. Now stick out your chest just a little. No need to look like a pigeon. But do push it a bit more than you think is normal. And now lift your chin up. Open your eyes and look around. Notice how you feel? You feel stronger, right? More aware? That's because you are! And you did that without breaking a sweat.

See how easy it is? And how powerful it can be?

You've picked up only three things so far:

1. Believe in yourself. Yes, you can!

2. Smile. It works wonders on you and everyone around you.

3. Stand tall, chin up, chest out, eyes up. Be the warrior.

Your challenge: Do it for a day. Be conscious of your posture throughout the entire day. Smile as often as possible. A small smile is fine. And say to yourself, "I can do this. It's easy."

Just try it. Remember, you promised to try and I promised to do the rest. So just try. Do it for a day.

# MAKE EYE CONTACT

So you're standing tall now. You feel bigger, look bigger, and will actually start acting bigger. Those are all good things.

Now be sure your eyes convey strength. Ever see a dog threaten another dog and the weaker one averts his eyes? It's a form of submission.

At the same time, you've probably had someone stare menacingly at you at some point. Maybe it was a parent? How did you feel? If you're like most people, you probably felt threatened. It's a natural response.

I want you to be more conscious of eye contact. Good eye contact conveys confidence. No eye contact is equivalent to submission.

With a little bit of effort, you will find you can indeed control where you look. Weak people invariably avoid eye contact. I want you to start practicing more eye contact. I don't want you to 'stare down' people like boxers about to start a match. Rather, refrain from the reflexive wayward glance.

Here's an interesting exercise: The next time you enter an elevator, make eye contact, nod your head "hello" and give a tiny smile. That says to the stranger, "I am confident. And I am not a threat."

Now, I'm not suggesting you should walk down the street or pull into and intersection and try to lock gazes with some stranger. That will surely get you in trouble.

Instead, let your eyes and the stranger's eyes meet briefly. Acknowledge each other. And then coolly look away. You are secure and you are nonthreatening. Let your eyes tell the story.

# BE PERSISTENT

You want to know why the Grand Canyon is so massive? Because water - among other things - is so persistent. It will keep wearing away at the rock, over and over again, until the rock eventually gives up.

Ever hear the phrase, "The squeaky wheel gets the grease?' Well, it's true. Maybe you know someone who asked for something over and over and over again. Annoying? Yes. Effective? Yes.

Persistence is key to every accomplishment. It doesn't matter if we're talking about good grades, dating, getting the job you want, or just learning something new. Persistence wins in the end.

You have to develop persistence. This one won't come over night. But you can start with yourself. Remember the smile exercise and the posture challenge? Amp it up. Instead of just doing it for one full day, do it tomorrow and the next day and the day after that. Adopt the secret black belt technique of persistence.

They say the thing we do over and over again is the thing we get good at. I am good at brushing my teeth because I have done it so

13

many times.  Get good at other things, too.
Just do it over and over again.  Stand tall, smile,
look around you.  Keep doing it.  Persistence
will get you there.

What scares me more than the fighter with
1000 techniques is the fighter that has practiced
one technique 1000 times.

## YOU GET WHAT YOU GIVE

You can't get something for nothing.
That's the way the universe works.  There's
always a cost or a price to be paid.  Either now
or later.

But that's a good thing.  Because it means
you can get something for something.  If you
want something, all you have to do is strive for
it.

One of my favorite quotes is from Thomas
Edison, "Opportunity comes dressed in
overalls and looks like hard work."

In my classes, I remind the students:
When you pray, don't forget to move your feet.
That means it's OK to want things.  But it's not
enough.  You actually have to do something
about.

14

This applies to things you may want, like a new car. It also applies to who or what you want to become. For example, if you want more friends, be friendly. Don't be a victim. If you want to be loved, be lovable. If you want people to support you, support them first.

They say you can have anything you want if you just give enough people what they want.

# SAVE MONEY

Money is not a cure-all, but it sure does help. It's possible to live without any money, but I don't think you want that life.

You will want to go to college. That takes money. You will want to travel. That takes money. You will want a nice home. Money. And you will want to take care of your family and the needy. Money.

The important thing is not how much money you make. It's how much you save. I may make a $1M per year, but spend $2M. That means I'm actually very poor - despite the big income.

Get in the habit of saving. Money in the bank will help you when you need it most.

And don't be afraid to invest your money. Learn the value of compounded interest. The sooner your money can be earning even more money, the better. And the sooner you can setup passive income, the better.

Money will help you secure a nice place to live, a rewarding profession, and the ability to pursue your interests. It supports your confidence. It's OK to start small. Just be persistent.

# STAY UPBEAT

Bad things happen. You will experience setbacks. Some may even seem overwhelming. But you have to find a way to push on. The sooner you can find some 'good' in a 'bad' situation and realign your emotions with the good, the sooner you will see sunshine.

You basically can choose the way you want to feel about something. Generally, it's a matter of perspective.

There are some things you can do to help you stay positive in the face of hardship. You should - of course - eat healthy, exercise, and get plenty of rest. All of those things will keep you happy. You should also surround yourself with people who bring out the best in you. Happy friends will bring you even more happiness. Music helps, too. Motivational music can put a bounce in your walk and help you feel better about yourself.

Whether it's reading, walking, or massage, find what works for you. Turn to that tool set on when you start feeling down.

Happy people exercise better judgment.

I like Winston Churchill's advice: "When you are going through hell, keep going."

## TRUST YOUR INSTINCTS

In the end, the one thing you must always be willing to do is trust your instincts. If something doesn't feel right, it probably isn't. If someone seems untrustworthy, he/she probably isn't.

As you grow older, you will develop a sense of right and wrong, good and bad. Cultivate your intuition. Learn to use your intellect and gut feelings in tandem to make wiser decisions.

Good judgment is the best way to avoid trouble. Ultimately, it's your best form of self defense.

## SPEAK UP FOR YOURSELF

Ever see a mean dog with a meek bark? No, mean dogs always have mean (loud) barks.

I'm not suggesting you should be mean. What I am saying is you need to speak up if you want people to take you seriously.

Can you imagine the President of the United States speaking with a muted voice? No one would elect him or her.

Learn to speak up for yourself. Raise the volume. Say it like you mean it. You don't have to yell. You just need to add a massive dose of confidence. Fake it if you have to. Faking it is perfectly OK. In fact, if you fake something enough times, you actually become really good at it.

Your challenge: Turn the volume up on your voice. Say it like you mean it - especially when it counts most.

Remember when your mom asked you to do something and you ignored her. And then she asked you again and you ignored her again. And then she raised her voice and suddenly you felt the fear of god and immediately did what she asked? Learn from your mom. Speak with authority.

The next time someone is picking on you, turn and tell that person to: "Knock it off!" Look him in the eye and say it with confidence and good, strong volume. Use a deeper voice. I guarantee you that person will just about pee his pants.

Don't forget your posture. If your voice is strong but your posture is week then it probably won't work. When you're telling

someone to knock it off, make sure your voice says, "No!" and your body says, "No!"

To make your body say, "No!" stand tall and raise your hand between you and the other person. Make sure your arm is fully extended. Put your hand in the other person's face, like you're signaling that person to 'Stop.' It works well.

# BE CAREFUL OF FLEAS

Hang out with smart people, and you will actually become smarter. Spend time with fitness freaks and you become more fit. It's true.

If your friends smoke, there's a high likelihood you will pick up that nasty habit. If your family and friends overeat, so will you. It's just a matter of time.

In my classes, we remind everyone two dogs share the same fleas. That means you are whom you spend time with.

The good news is you can choose your friends. You can decide.

So if you want to do better in school, befriend the students who do well. If you want to get more fit, sit with the athletes.

# AVOID DANGEROUS SITUATIONS

That's sage advice. We've probably heard our parents say that a gazillion times, and yet we still do dumb things. Why? Mostly because we just don't think bad things will happen to us. Be careful about developing a sense of immortality. Yes, you can get hurt. And yes, you can die.

The best self-defense is staying out of situations where you might have to defend yourself. I'm not suggesting you live like a hermit in your home and avoid all risk. I'm saying there are plenty of stupid things we are tempted to do. Here's the short list of stuff you should not do - ever:

- Abuse drugs and alcohol
- Text while driving
- Walk at through gang-ridden areas
- Hop in the car with a reckless and/or inexperienced driver
- Driving while tired
- Go anywhere with strangers

## GET FIT

Poor health is exhausting. It tires you, wastes your money and zaps your time. And burdens your families and friends.

Think how easily you can get up right now, walk to the bathroom, and come back. Now imagine you have to go to the bathroom, but you can't move your legs. Your arms are fine, but your legs don't work. Go ahead. Crawl to the bathroom.

Your health is the one thing you can rightfully claim as your own. Don't squander it on poor eating habits and a sedentary lifestyle. You don't want to be the guy crawling to the bathroom.

Instead, take an interest in feeling healthy and alert. Find some activity you enjoy. Learn about nutrition and eat well.

I once saw two people fighting. One was a thief, running from a security guard. The thief was fit and could run like the wind. The security guard was obese and had a tough time jogging. Guess what happened. Nothing. The thief got away. Didn't even have to run that fast. It was comic.

But imagine it's you and a bad guy. And it's your turn to run - away from danger. Can you do it? How far can you sprint? Find a football field and run that distance full speed. If you can do the whole 100 yards, you are in good shape. If you're limping along after the first 40 yards, you need to get fit.

A real street fight is like sprinting - it's anaerobic. It's not sustainable. You won't be able to bring in enough oxygen after a while and will have to take a break. That's why it's so critical to be in good shape. Good technique + good fitness = good fighter.

You don't want to face a threatening situation in poor health. Be a warrior and get fit.

# DON'T LOOK FOR TROUBLE

This message is similar to the fleas. If you go looking for trouble, you will find it. And in most cases, it doesn't end well for everyone involved.

I often remind my students of the champion fighter in San Francisco. He was leaving his school one evening when he saw another car back into his parked car. The car took off, and the fighter chased after him. When he caught up to the car at a nearby intersection, the fighter started pounding on the window. Startled and afraid, the driver pulled out a gun and shot the fighter dead. What would the fighter give just to be alive today? What do you think he would tell you the next time you feel like being a hero?

I know what he would say. He would say, "Be a hero. If you see something wrong, call the police. But don't be an idiot and get yourself killed."

Boys, you especially have to remember this one. Testosterone will make you want to do some pretty stupid things. Use your brain, not your fists. Don't go looking for trouble.

# BE AWARE

Most martial arts teachers will tell you this is one of the most important self-defense measures: awareness.

I had a driver's ed teacher in high school. He loved to ask, "What color is the car behind you?" but you weren't allowed to look. He was trying to instill the habit of looking around - including looking in the rear view mirror.

Being aware of what's behind you is a habit. You have to practice it. Start with your eyes. Get in the habit of looking around you. I always look left, then right, then behind, and then all over again.

Pilots are trained to scan the cockpit gauges and then look left to right in the sky and then back to the cockpit gauges...and then back to the sky...in an ongoing clockwise pattern.

It's especially important to 'look around' whenever you enter a room or a building, or when you're entering or leaving your car.

One black belt trick is to use the reflection off glass surfaces to see what's happening behind you. When I approach a glass door, I can see what's happening behind me.

Am I paranoid? No. Just curious. Aware.

## AVOID FIGHTING

I am more impressed by the number of fights a person has avoided than the number of fights that person has 'won.'

Fighting - with punches, weapons, etc. - is dangerous business. I am going to teach you how to protect yourself, but as a rule of thumb, if you can walk (or run!) away from confrontation then you should.

Why? Because you can get seriously hurt. I can tell you stories of experienced martial artists who elected to fight and ended up dead. Do you think if they could do it over, they would have eagerly jumped into those fights again? Probably, not. They would choose life over death. Bottom line is, you never know who carries a gun or a knife, or who might suddenly jump out of the bushes to gang up on you.

So, when you have a choice, choose peace. Use humor, street savvy, or whatever to avoid fighting.

However, when you don't have choice, when you are in real danger, I want you to fight to win. I want you to fight dirty.

# FIGHT DIRTY

You've seen boxing on TV and maybe you've watched some MMA fighting on YouTube. Those matches all have rules and those fighters must follow those rules. For example, you never see anyone get kicked in the nuts in a boxing match even though it's a very effective technique. You don't see pinching, hair pulling, spitting, eye-gouging, name-calling, etc. Those things just aren't allowed.

If you are in serious danger, if someone is really trying to hurt you, I want you to escape as quickly and as efficiently as possible using all you've got.

So get the whole rule thing out of your head. When you're defending yourself, your job is to win. Period. Don't even think about boxing the other person or wrestling the guy down to the ground. If you can't avoid the fight and someone is really intent on hurting you, then I want you to get comfortable with the idea that you will have to hurt that person...badly.

There's only one person going to the hospital. You or him. You decide.

# GET COMFORTABLE

# CAUSING PAIN

We don't like receiving pain. And we don't like causing pain. This is perfectly natural and is actually a good thing. It helps preserve a sense of order in our world.

But if you're in danger, you must be willing to do what it takes to survive. If someone's trying to abduct you, aren't you going to muster the strength and will to end the situation as quickly as you can? Of course you will.

If you can run, run.  If you can scream and draw attention to yourself, do it.  Do what it takes.  And if you have to poke out someone's eye, or stab that person in the neck with a pen, then that's what I want you to do with complete commitment.

When you deliver pain, do it without hesitation and without restraint.  I want you channel all your fear and all your anger and everything you've got into the techniques I am about to teach you.  Inside you is a tiger.  It is sleeping.  But when the time comes for you to fight, I want you to wake up that tiger and let it destroy your assailant.

Now, I am **not** suggesting you need to kill your opponent.  In most cases, you just need to incapacitate the person.  I will teach you how to do it quickly and with minimal effort so you can run to safety.

Note:  Safety is generally where there are adults.  Always flee to public areas.  The bad guys hate attention.

# TRAINING MANUAL

**IMPORTANT**: Everything I'm teaching you here is **special and secret**. It's only to be used when someone is REALLY trying to hurt you. If someone is trying to hurt you **and you cannot run away**, you have to protect yourself. If someone just comes over and calls you a name or flicks your ear - that doesn't give you the right to punch them or kick them. You have to be responsible for what you do. If you break someone's arm, the police will want to know why and you better have a good reason for it.

P.S. Please feel free to practice these techniques on your dad. But leave your little brother alone.

*** 

## *Punch*

The punch is over-rated. Everyone attempts it but few people are actually good at it. The problem is two-fold. First, most beginners make a poor fist. It's not tight enough and not straight enough. In fact, it's not uncommon for people to break their hands when using punches in real fights. Ever wonder why boxers wear gloves? Well, to protect their hands from injury.

The second reason why punching can be ineffective as a fighting tool for novices is this: aim. Untrained punches go all over the place. Few actually hit the intended target. That's a lot of wasted energy and if you've ever been in a real fight, you know how tiring it can get real quick. Fighting is basically an aerobic activity, like sprinting. You can't do it for long. It's just too exhausting.

Let me teach you how to punch.

1. Make a good fist. Pull your fingers in as tightly as possible and lock your thumb over the top.
2. Make it harder than the thing you are hitting. Your fist has got to be super hard...or your hand will break when it hits the target.
3. Keep your wrist straight...or it will break when you hit the target.
4. Use the two main knuckles as the weapon.

31

5. Aim for softer tissue, like nose, mouth, chin, etc. Do not aim for skull, chest, leg, etc. Those targets don't damage quickly enough. As I tell my students, punch me in the chest and I will laugh. Punch me in the nose and I will cry like a baby. By the way, the nose is an excellent target. It protrudes from the face, so it's hard to miss. It's soft, so it's safer on my hands. It breaks easily and thus is nicely debilitating. And it bleeds easily and abundantly, which always scares the geebeez out of the attacker. If you bonk someone really hard on the nose, their eyes will tear up, they won't see straight, they bleed and they will be scared. Note: Watch out for blood on the ground. It's very slippery.

6. Punch through the target. This is very important. You must extend your punch through the nose and through the head. I like to imagine my arm going all the way to the horizon behind the target. This ensures my punch destroys everything in its path.

7. Punch multiple times. One punch is often not enough. Get in the habit of throwing three combinations: jab, cross, jab. Repeat.

To learn more and to watch a free instructional video on proper punching, go to: www.smartkarate.com/self-defense-for-kids

## *Combat Slap*

This is one is my favorite. It's easy to learn, easy to do and very effective. Basically, all you have to do is slap the attacker in the face. But to make it work, there are a few things you should do:

1. Use your whole body.
2. Strike with the heel of your palm.
3. Aim for the juicy targets, like the temple, the jaw bone (below the ear), nose, mouth and chin.
4. Go through the target. This is very important.
5. Follow up immediately with more strikes. The first slap will stun the attacker. Don't give him a chance to regain his composure. Continue striking until you have a chance to run away.

## *Palm Heel*

If you open your hand and thrust the heel of your palm forward, you've done the palm heel. It's devastating when used on the fragile parts of the face, like the nose, mouth and chin. The key is to flex your hand upwards so only the bottom part of your palm hits the target. Make the hand as rigid as possible, shoot as straight as possible (as you would if you were punching) and blast through the target.

Like the combat slap and every other strike, it's very important to go through the target. Don't stop at the surface. The faster you accelerate the strike, the more force you generate. It's important to be fast.

Palm heel is one of the first techniques we teach. It's safe and effective. Anyone can do it. Remember, it works best on the face.

See it at: www.smartkarate.com/self-defense-for-kids

## *Hair Pull*

You know how luggage has handles? Well, people do too. It's called hair. Always feel free to grab a fist full of your attacker's hair and pull it as violently as you can. It's a great way to gain control of that person.

To do it right, you need to grab as much as possible as close to the scalp as possible. I like to quickly thread close to the head. This ensures good volume and good surface area.

After you've got the hair, you can punch the attacker, slap him, poke him in the eyes, yank him to the ground, pull him off of you, etc. He's all yours. Just be careful of his free hands and do your business quickly and without hesitation.

## *Eye Poke*

Need to stop an attacker much bigger and stronger than you? Poke him in the eye. It's as simple as that. It will stop him in his tracks and make him cry like a baby. It will also severely impair his field of depth. To see for yourself, close one eye and try to reach for something, anything. It's tough with one eye. Now imagine someone shoves their fingers deep into your eye socket. It would be very painful and very debilitating.

Like most of the things I am teaching you, you have to do it with full commitment. I realize it's horrible to think about crushing someone's eye like a squished grape. But when you're in danger, you have to be willing to inflict enormous amounts of pain, without hesitation.

There's only one person going to the hospital, and you get to decide who that is. You or him.

If you're in danger and you have a chance to poke the attacker's eye, do it. And then get the heck out of there.

36

## Finger Break

Fingers break like chicken bones. If you can grab one, bend it backwards with as much force as you can muster. It will dislocate and break with very little effort and will send your attacker wailing on the ground.

To break a finger, grab one with your whole hand and then break the finger with full force. I like to yell or scream when doing this one. It gives me more power and scares the attacker. Yelling or screaming while attacking also makes it easier to hurt someone.

## Shin Kick

Martial arts movies are great. I love the flying kicks and the fancy moves. Those actors are especially talented and it's always thrilling to watch them - especially in slow motion!

But most fights are pretty simple affairs. There's a quick exchange of blows and - in most cases - it's over. You seldom see two people squared off, fighting toe to toe, like prime time boxers. And you never see the kind of fighting action found on the movie screen.

I like a scene from Indiana Jones, where our hero is suddenly facing a very skilled and flamboyant swordsman. Remember that one, where the bad guy jumps out and starts doing all these ornate sword moves, showing his skill? And then with little thought, Indy pulls out his gun and shoots the guy. Game over.

If you ever have to fight, think Indiana Jones. No, I don't mean shoot the person. I simply mean find the one technique you can do quickly and easily that would end the whole thing. The best fighters aren't sweating when the fight is over. The worst fighter has black eyes and bloodied faces.

Practice your shin kick. Get good at it. Find a wall or a tree and kick it over and over again until you feel you could fire off one of those unglamorous yet very effective babies in time of need. Note: Unless you are wearing steel-tipped shows, you will need to pull your toes back when hitting the target. Keep the foot horizontal and perpendicular to the striking surface, but pull the toes up and out of the way.

By the way, if you have a great kick but lousy aim, your kick won't be worth 10 cents! Find a spot on the wall and hit that one spot over and over again. Accuracy is key. Take your time and slow down the kick if you have to. Better to develop focus first and then add power. Watch how to do it properly at: www.smartkarate.com/self-defense-for-kids

## *Neck Strike*

Your neck is one of the most vulnerable areas of your body. Don't let anyone touch it - except (someday) your mate, of course.

If someone reaches for your neck, move away. Knock their hands away if necessary. Just don't let anyone mess with your neck, even if they are goofing around.

The reasons are clear: Break the neck and risk paralysis. Choke the neck and say hello to unconsciousness, maybe even death.

But whatever is dangerous for you is usually dangerous for other humans, too. In other words, you can teach yourself effective techniques by exploring your own body. Poke yourself in the eye. Hurts, doesn't it? Well, that's precisely why you can and should use the same technique on your assailant.

So let's say you are in a life-threatening situation and you do have the opportunity to attack the neck. Here's what you can do:

- Hit the Adam's Apple as hard as you can with whatever you've got. You can use your fist, the ridge of your hand, a stick...anything blunt and solid. In most cases, the bad guy will drop in pain, giving you plenty of time to get away (always run towards a public space where there are adults. Bad guys will seldom follow you there.)

- Choke. If you have to do it, then do it. But don't stop choking until the bad guy goes unconscious. And even then hold it for another 15 seconds. This will ensure the bad guy is unconscious. If you continue to hold the choke well beyond the 15 seconds of unconsciousness, then you run the risk of killing the person or a least causing serious brain damage. The police are going to want to know why you had to kill someone. You better have a good reason!

## Groin strike

Men have been trying to protect their groins since they were boys. And some have developed pretty good reflexes as a result. In fact, you can fake a kick to a man's groin and in almost all cases he will reflexively drop his hands down to protect himself. Just follow up with a few strikes to the face (because his hands are down near his belt) and then get out of there.

Still, the groin is an excellent target. And just like any other part of the body, you can hit with just about anything, including your fist, your foot, a pencil and a baseball bat.

As always, be sure to strike through the target. Don't just 'slap' the surface. If you want to cause pain AND damage, always go through the thing you are hitting. As a rule of thumb, aim for a spot 5 inches deeper than the target. This will ensure the maximum force and thus an effective technique.

41

## *Knee break*

I love high kicks. There's nothing prettier than kicking high.

But low kicks are easier to do in street clothes, don't require any pre-stretching, and are very, very effective.

When you are confronted with a bad guy, all you need to do is disable that person. That's it! No prolonged fighting, no exchange of blows, just one decisive technique to prevent that person from following you.

A good, strong kick to the knee will get the job done. Ever see a one-legged person run fast? Neither have I.

When kicking the knee, concentrate on just two things: hitting the target (not that easy) and going through the target. If you make contact just above or below the knee, your kick won't do damage. Aim for the front of the kneecap - using a front kick - or the sides of the knee using a roundhouse kick (instep) or a side kick (bottom of heel.)

Remember, the goal is to disable and get out of there.

By the way, you can use any object to damage the knee. It doesn't have to your foot. A baseball bat works extremely well.

## *Pinch*

It's easy to do, discreet, and very effective.

There are a few different types of pain. For example, there's pain of the heart, like unrequited love or the death of a pet. Then there's bearable physical pain, like a paper cut or the burn you feel on your 60th pushup.

And then there's reflexive, unbearable pain, line a burn or a paper cut. For obvious reasons, the human body is conditioned to instantly move away from unbearable pain. For example, it's very difficult and takes tremendous mental strength to keep your finger firmly planted on a hot iron. Try it.

So, to pinch like a rock star, first realize not all pinches are equal. Pinch my cheek, and I will laugh. Pinch the area under my bicep, and I will cry like a baby.

In general, to cause maximum unbearable pain, choose an area of the body that typically doesn't get a lot of natural sunlight, pinch the surface, outer-skin area (not the whole muscle), and squeeze and twist that thing like you want to rip it off the body. Don't be shy. Good pinches are very violent endeavors. Do not hold back.

We have highlighted a few areas that work well. (See additional information and techniques at www.smartkarate.com/self-defense-for-kids) But like all things, you can teach yourself. The next time you're by yourself, take a few minutes and explore your own body. Pinch here, pinch there. Find the good spots. And pinch just a little, or a lot, and figure out what works.

If it hurts, it works.

By the way, the pinch is a fun one to practice on friends and family. Just tell them you are reading this book and learning how to do it right. Tell them you need a partner and it won't hurt that much. Have fun with it.

## *Bite*

I'm not a big fan of biting, only because I don't want to ingest the bad guy's fluids. You never know what that person's got.

But if you're in a life or death situation, and biting is the only immediate option, then do it with gusto. Basically, all you have to do is bite whatever is in front of your mouth. Don't worry. It will work.

We are primal animals. We know how to bite and we know we don't want to be bitten. Use that innate fear to your advantage.

Again, only bite if you have to. And when you do, be sure to spit out whatever comes off - because it will.


## *Stomp*


Some of the strongest muscles in your body are your butt muscles: the gluteus maximus muscle, gluteus medius muscle and gluteus minimus muscle. They carry the weight of your body up and down stairs every day.

So it's not surprising that the stomp is actually a very powerful technique. Think about it. You may not be able to crush a can with your hands. But you can surely do it with a stomp.

When you do the stomp, be sure you use the bottom of your heel. You want to create a hard surface. And also make sure you raise the knee (we call it chambering) as high as possible. Now accelerate the stomp as much as possible. Force - after all - is the product of mass and acceleration. So the more you accelerate, the more devastating the technique. Aim for the top of the bad guy's foot.

Remember to smash through it. I always like to think I am extending my foot to the center of the earth, and the bad guy's foot just happens to be in the way! Works every time.

If you're wearing high heels, use them, the more weapons, the better.

## *Spit*

My students (and their parents!) are always so alarmed when I introduce this technique. Spitting? That's so gross. And that's why it works so well.

What's the one thing that repulses everyone? The disgusting stuff. If you act crazed, smearing poop on your face, people will run. I guarantee it. No one wants to fight a sickening lunatic. It's too unsettling.

You can use that to your advantage. A good spit in the face of the bad guy works every time - but only for a few seconds.

Here's how you do it: Imagine someone is very close to your face and that person is obviously intent on hurting you. Quickly gather as much saliva as you can and blow the whole load all over his face. Be super intense about it. You get only one chance.

If you are like me, people just don't go around spitting in my face. That means I am completely unaccustomed to it. Spit in my face and I will be paralyzed with disbelief for 2-3 seconds. That's plenty of time for you to high tail it out of there.

## Use weapons

At my school we make a point of practicing group attacks, like 2 on 1. Fighting one on one is easy. Fighting two or more on one is tougher.

Facing a much larger/stronger opponent is also very difficult. David and Goliath is a myth because the smaller guy actual won. In real life, it's the other way around. The big guy wins.

But the one equalizer is weapons. They are all around you. You just need to use them. For example, Starbucks coffee in the face? Very effective. Chair against the head? Very effective. Umbrella into the sternum? Yes.

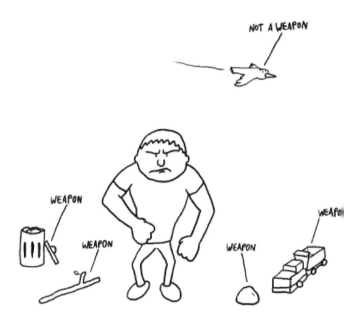

Anything - everything - is a weapon. You just need to make it one. It's up to you.

Exercise: Put this book down for a minute and take inventory around you. Where are the weapons? Can this book be used as a weapon? Of course, it can.

Whenever you are fighting for your life, use the stuff around you to disable your attacker. Fight dirty. Be decisive.

## *Feign submission*

This technique is a little tricky, but it does work in some severe situations. If you're ever facing overwhelming odds, you may be able to escape later if you appear to give in now. For example, when attacked by a bear, you should never try to run away. Bears are too fast. You can't outrun them.

Nor can you stand toe-to-toe with a bear and beat it up. Bears are just too big and strong for most humans.

What you should do, though, is curl into a ball and play dead. The bear will swat you and may even bite, but if you just play dead, the bear will recognize you are no longer a threat and leave.

If you and I are about to fight, and I adopt an aggressive fight stance, chances are you will do the same. I raise my guard, you raise yours. I lower my guard, you lower yours.

So you can diffuse a high-tension situation by assuming non-threatening body language. You can even cower - all with the intention of getting the bad guy to lower his guard. Once his guard is dropped, you can attack him very aggressively and/or find an opportunity to escape.

## Verbal assault

The bad guys know words really do hurt. They know if they hurl really nasty, violent words at a target, the victim will likely feel very intimidated and less likely to fight. It's abusive and it's very effective.

If you're unaccustomed to verbal assault, your first experience with it will probably be unforgettable.

The only way to get comfortable with verbal attacks is to practice it. And it's hard to find someone who is willing to intimidate you with vicious language. But I put together a video for you. You can watch it here: www.smartkarate.com/self-defense-for-kids

You should learn how to turn it on, too. Remember, what works against you, also works for you. So if verbal assault is intimidating for you, then it's intimidating for others. You can use it to your advantage.

In any case, just recognize verbal attacks for what they really are: An attempt by savvy fighters to intimidate you and break your will to fight. If you don't let it get to you, it won't have an effect on you.

## Knives are worse than guns

I don't care how good of a martial artist you are, if you're ever facing a knife fight, run. Because you will get cut if you don't.

In Hawaii, there was a 7th degree black belt, very accomplished martial artist, who squared off with another guy with a knife. The black belt died at the scene.

Knife wounds are serious and require immediate medical attention. Five minutes of excessive bleeding will send you into shock and eventually death.

As a rule of thumb, if it looks like a knife fight, run like the wind.

If you can't run, then grab whatever weapon you can (like a baseball bat) to equalize the fight. Keep your eyes on the blade the entire time, and use low kicks (not high kicks). It's harder for the bad cut to cut your leg when you're kicking low.

As for gun-wielding bad guys, you don't want to fight them either. If you get held up at gunpoint, give the bad guy what he wants. Your wallet? No problem. Your car keys? No problem. In each case, throw the item near his feet. Don't hand it to him. Keep your distance. And get ready to run.

Believe it or not, it's very hard to shoot a moving target, even at close range. In fact, studies show there's only a 4% hit rate when the good guy high tails it out of there in a diagonal or zigzagging fashion.

## *Block what should be blocked*

The movies always show the martial artist blocking everything that comes near him. You don't have to do it. For one, it's hard to block everything. Two, it gets tiring very quickly. Better to conserve your energy.

If something is coming toward you, get out of the way. If you can't get out of the way, then block it. In general, keep your hands up, your chin down and your elbows in. This will help you guard your vitals, like your face, neck, chest, ribs, stomach, etc. If there's a kick or a punch, let your guard position absorb the blow. Keep you guard up and rotate your body to deflect blows. Don't start moving your arms in a wild windmill type fashion hoping to catch every attack like a Jett Li. It doesn't work that way.

Best to keep your distance. Don't be anywhere where the punch is at.

## *Keep your balance*

Good guard dogs are trained to attack in tandem. One dog goes high and the other goes low. The objective is to knock you down, where you are less able to fight - let alone get away.

Balance is key to good punches, kicks, blocks and evasive maneuvers.

If your balance is poor, you are more susceptible to being tripped, thrown and knocked over. And just like the case of the dogs, on the ground is the last place you want to be.

Balance is developed over time. But there are a few things you can do. Keep your feet apart. Whenever you cross your legs, you run the risk of getting tripped.

Distribute your weight evenly. If you have too much weight on your front foot, I will sweep it and you will fall like a rock.

Bend your knees a bit. This engages the leg muscles and the butt muscles. It gives you the ability to shift positions quickly.

Keep your weight on the front part of your foot - not the heel. Think about it. When you sprint, you use the front part (the ball) of your foot. Stay light-footed.

Lower your center of gravity. This helps keep you from being bowled over.

Stay relaxed. Stay flexible. Absorb blows. But keep your feet firmly planted. Breathe.

## *Never go willingly*

The bad guy will always want to bring you somewhere else. Don't go. Believe me, the bad guy will never bring you any place good.

If you're at knifepoint or gunpoint and told to hop in the car, for example, just run like crazy. Fight for your life if you have to. But don't ever get in the car.

As discussed early, the bad guy never likes attention. Chances are, he will refrain from creating any commotion in public. That's why it's better to be in public than in private. In public, at least there may be someone to come to your rescue.

If and when you do run, always run towards other people. Head for the public spaces. The bad guy will seldom follow you there.

## *Use barriers*

Remember, distance is your friend. Always stay far enough away from danger.

Barriers can help create distance. If you are threatened, use the pole, the tree, or the car to keep the bad guys at bay.

One thing to keep in mind: It's hard to outrun a cheetah. But you can definitely out-turn one. If someone is chasing you, and that person is faster than you, just turn quickly. Think about it. A jet cannot turn quickly. Why? Because it's too fast. In order for a jet to turn quickly, it actually has to slow down first.

# Summary

In summary, there is no one easy and simple prescription to avoid bullying or being picked on. The overall goal is to be strong inside and to know that you will face tough times and that you will be OK. Also, please know that you are not alone. Whenever you face challenges, it's wise to seek help and support of others. Never hesitate to speak with your parents, teachers, peers, and police. I am always here to help. Feel free to reach out. E-mail me at james@smartkarate.com

# ABOUT THE AUTHOR

James Kerr has 30 years experience in the martial arts and has served as an AAU (American Athletics Union) certified martial arts coach and tournament judge. He has a 4th degree black belt in Hapkido and a 1st degree black belt in Taekwondo In addition to founding SmartKarate, he owns IT company SuperGeeks.

Made in the USA
Charleston, SC
13 September 2012